BETTERNESS AT INVESTING

ß✧ð

The art of creating wealth.

ß✧ð

BOB DENEEN

Copyright 2010, Robert N. Deneen

Published by bobdeneen.com
http://www.bobdeneen.com

Printed in the United States of America.
by CreateSpace®
Charleston, SC
www.createspace.com/344586

Library of Congress Control Number: 2010905207
Deneen, Bob (Robert N.) 1928-
BETTERNESS AT INVESTING ---- creating wealth
Includes bibliographical, indexed references, and investing worksheets:
    1. Attitude 2. Strategy 3. Management

ISBN: 1-451-599323

EAN: 978-1-451-59932-9

Acknowledgement

Betterness At Investing is dedicated to my mother, Verna Deneen Lindsay, who taught herself about investing and managed her investments until she died at the age of 94.

She bought a home, sent me to college, and bought a car with stock earnings – a huge accomplishment for a single working mother.

When unable to get answers from co-workers or friends, she went to the library to read *The Value Line Investment Surveys®* and the *Wall Street Journal*.

She attended a night school course to learn how to become a "buy & hold" investor – which she accomplished on the salary of a secretary during WWII.

It was late in my life when I learned the details of her investing experiences. Extensive research revealed that her strategies were the same as leading investment experts -- Graham, Buffet, and Lynch -- whose strategies are reviewed in this book.

If a single mother, working at a minimum wage, can create wealth from stock investments, so can you.

CONTENTS

Section II -- next page

ೞ✧ೠ

> **The greatest discovery is that humans can alter their lives by altering their attitudes.**
>
> Albert Schweitzer

BETTERNESS AT INVESTING

CR✧ED

BOB DENEEN

SECTION I

INVESTING FOR WEALTH

INTRODUCTION

The opportunity to create wealth in the stock market is available to anyone with the right mindset. The right attitude is more important than market's status. Doubt and fear are obstacles to creating wealth.

The right mindset is difficult for people easily influenced by sensationalist news, and people who doubt that stocks are the best way to create wealth. People with positive mind-sets know that stock investing is not without occasional trepidation, but can be profitable.

As for control, investors too often neglect investments and are satisfied with mediocre results. They don't aim for higher returns – for at least the average of 11 % per year.

While primarily designed for novice investors, this book introduces basic strategies to maximize investment wealth. *Worksheets* are included to help manage investments effectively and profitably by concentrating on:
- ✓ *facts – and not myths*
- ✓ *companies rather than the market.*
- ✓ *percentage of gain rather than dollar amount.*
- ✓ *possible gains rather than average gains.*

The term *"betterness"* means to *achieve peak performance* – which anyone can accomplish if they seek it.

Anyone can create wealth...............
What you seek, you shall find. (Matthew 7:7)

Rational investors enjoy safe and profitable investing by owning growth stocks or mutual funds that have the potential to create wealth. They are easy to find -- this book shows where to find them.

<u>Betterness At Investing</u> represents thousands of hours of research discovering how expert investors created their wealth – for example:
- ✓ During market downturns, they invest to increase holdings and at lower cost.
- ✓ They enjoy higher gains than the general market's 100 year average return of 11%/year.
- ✓ They invest in *growth companies.*
- ✓ They *maximize the total return* of investments.
- ✓ They ignore myths.

Although *Betterness At Investing* describes how to become a profitable investor, the information in this book is useless if not put into action.

CB ✧ BD

Chapter 1

Investor Mindset

A negative mind will keep you poor. A positive action-oriented mindset will make you wealthy.

Common myths prevent people from investing. Rather than thinking for themselves, amateur investors react to irrational myths. They fear minor risks and doubt the huge potential to create wealth.

The right mindset is not a matter of intelligence. According to Dr. Edward deBono Intelligent people can fail to think effectively as when they tend to react rather than reason.

Dr. deBono, a renowned thinking expert, says *intelligence is a burden when it is suspicious rather than inquisitive*.

People become trapped in mediocrity by doubt and inaction. Suspicious people harbor fears about potentially profitable investments. They do not believe *they* can create wealth using easy-to-learn tactics.

Because they doubt that they can be successful investors, negative thinkers don't bother to try to learn how to invest successfully.

Sensation seeking media, brokers, and dubious economists dissuade novices from finding the truth by spreading myths and causing potential investors to believe that:

- ☞ Stocks are not safe investments
- ☞ All investments are the same
- ☞ Investing in stocks requires lots of money
- ☞ Many different companies must be owned
- ☞ Only *experts* know what to invest in
- ☞ Higher than average returns are not possible

Myth: *Stocks are not safe investments*:
This is nonsense! People who think stocks are not safe ignore the facts. They have not studied profitable investors or *Value Line Surveys*®. They do not *think* for themselves. They allow a single negative topic override positive facts.

Myth: *All investments are the same*:
False! Individuals, institutions, and funds invest differently. Young people invest differently than seniors. Institutions invest differently than individuals. *Investor* is a broad term. This text focuses on the do-it-yourself sole decision-maker.

Individuals should not attempt to compete with or use the same strategy as financial institutions or professional day-traders. They have super computer investing power that uses artificial intelligence to influence trades. This power has influenced markets to react with irrational behavior as in the 2010 market gyrations. However, d-i-y investors can succeed using simple investment strategies.

Myth: *Investing in stocks requires lots of money.*
False! As little as $25 to $50 can be invested to grow to thousands of dollars. $25 monthly deposits can create million dollar portfolios within a lifetime. This is achieved by taking advantage of no-cost tactics available to every investor that seeks higher returns.

Myth: *Many different companies must be owned.*
Partially False! The myth of "diversity" was created by brokers. You cannot diversify with small amounts of money. A small portfolio of five or six companies (in different industries) can grow profitably. Owning more than can be effectively managed is a not wise. Brokers promote diversity to sell stock and to offset bad advice.

Myth: Only *experts* know what stocks to invest in:
Wrong! In 2003, NY State convicted several brokerage firms and funds of intentionally misleading clients. *The Individual Investors Association* discovered that individual investors do better than broker assisted investors. Jargon and broker hype cause investing to seem complex and mysterious, which it is not. Listen to the advice of an honest broker, but make your own decisions.

Myth: *High returns are not possible:*
Wrong! A number of stocks, and mutual funds, outperform the market. The market average is always lower from the multitude of slow growth stocks. Only 100 growth firms lead the market – and these are included in several mutual funds. Whereas the general market average is 11%, annual averages of 17% and higher are possible.

Not a Myth:

Investors who don't sell during a bear-market support the market, whereas institutional computer-trading causes havoc. Perhaps a national agency is needed to protect individual investors from the maneuverings of major financial institutions.

Positive Outlook

Jonathan Clements admonished investors to exploit opportunities (Buffalo News, 5/18/03): *Either you get it or you don't. Whenever an investment falls in value, your first instinct should be to buy more. Yet most folks don't react this way.* Clements reminded readers that *people run to buy bargains in material things but shun bargains in stocks*!

Baby-boomers own the largest segment of investments. They will inherit a trillion dollars and become a new and greater economic force. The impact of this huge wealth will benefit the economy more than any government action.

Baby-boomers will be able to withdraw cash and remain heavily invested. Their spending on goods and services will boost the economy with more money being spent for food, clothing, medicine, homes, travel, and taxes. Businesses must support this growth in order to survive. The need for buildings, workers, machinery, and supplies will increase.

In 2008, the havoc created by spurious financial dealings on Wall Street caused people to react negatively about the future. They forgot that downturns are always temporary and that most of the time the market is bullish.

For over 100 years, economic growth has been consistent --
yet people think negatively about the future that will
exceed past performance -- serving the needs of a growing
robust economy. Trust reality.

**Whatever your financial status, you are nowhere near
your potential for creating more wealth.**

To find wealth, seek it.

Summary of Chapter 1 – Investor Mindset

- Think positively about growth and profit potential.

- Believe in your ability to create wealth.

- Your mind can make you rich or keep you poor. Think negatively and miss the opportunity to create more wealth.

- Take the steps that achieve betterness at investing – exploit time and the compounding of value.

- Trust facts. Ignore the myths that interfere with the rational and profitable investing.

- Fact: Do-it-yourself investors can outperform managed investments. Become your own investment expert.

ଓ✧ଯ

Chapter 2

PROFITABLE STOCK INVESTING

The purpose of stock investing is to *create wealth* by putting money to work -- for your benefit.

Profitable investing is not complicated – only people make it so. Keep it simple, use the KISS principle and prosper.

To create wealth *buy & hold* shares of *growth companies* and *maximize the total return on each equity*. By managing reward against risk, experienced investors are able to produce a *high total return* – which is the total of price appreciation, dividend yield, and compounded value.

Long-term growth is dependent on a company's <u>products</u>, <u>commercial market, and management</u>. Effectively managed corporations excel in stock value because of their ability to consistently grow in marketshare and profit.

Buy a stock as if it's your only investment. But, "buy & hold" does not mean "buy & forget". Routine monitoring assures that shares remain good to hold.

Risk is lowered and reward boosted by selecting proven-to-grow equities listed in *Value Line Investment Surveys*® --

and by adhering to *The Rules of Profitable Investing©*. Maximum returns are possible when investors apply the strategies proven profitable by successful investors such as Warren Buffett, Benjamin Graham, Peter Lynch and others.

There is always the risk that a stock will not perform as desired, but research and portfolio management will reduce this risk. The potential for growth is also limited when goals are set too low.

Fact: *Common stocks, including some mutual funds, are the best way to create wealth.* When properly managed, common stocks are safe and sure investments. In spite of occasional downturns, the economy continually grows because people, businesses, and organizations, need goods and services.

At any one time, 100 stocks, and a few funds, are good long-term investments. Investors can find these stocks in *Value Line®*. Risk is reduced and reward maximized by applying the following rules:

Rules for Profitable Investing©
1. Have an investment plan
2. Invest in growth companies
3. Make your own decisions/exploit information
4. Maximize *total return*
5. Monitor/measure performance
6. Adjust holdings -- if potential changes

Rule #1 -- Have an investment plan:

Preparation is vital. A well-planned portfolio increases the potential for greater profit. Investors without a plan miss opportunities to *maximize total return*. Plans define goals and how they will be achieved -- as shown in the next chapter.

Rule # 2 -- Buy proven growth companies:

New companies lack proof of safety and growth. Companies with <u>years of growth</u> have less risk and greater reward. Be safe, own shares of companies in business more than 25 years -- as listed in *Value Line's Growth Companies®* -- as shown in Chapter 7.

Rule # 3 -- Make your own decisions:

It's your money; you decide what to buy and sell. Seek advice but also do your own research. With the right information you can manage as will as anyone Build confidence with a <u>practice portfolio</u>.

Rule # 4 -- Maximize total return:

Buying stock on a schedule <u>lowers the average cost of shares</u>. Money deposited into Dividend Reinvestment Plans (DRIPs) accumulate shares at lower cost. Routine deposits can grow to thousands of dollars when compounded – usually in fifteen years and thereafter.

Tactics that maximize total return -- DCA, DRIPS, Splits, Yield, and compounding -- are available to all investors.

A portfolio will naturally grow in value with the accumulation of more and more shares. Value increases by continually acquiring more shares, buying shares at the lowest possible cost, and by maximizing total return.

Any increase in the value of shares – even little -- increases the total value of holdings – which will later multiply in value by the magic of compounding.

Rule # 5 -- Monitor and measure performance:

Qualify performance in percentages. What is measured well gets done well. Don't measure only in dollars. Measure growth as a *percentage* of gain. Monitoring assures that investments haven't turned sour.

If confronted by a negative assessment repeat the selection process – explore *Value Line* before making a hold/sell decision

Rule # 6 -- Adjust holdings when necessary:

Resist hanging on to holdings that have no prospect of improving. Investors intent on maximizing total return can't afford to fall in love with their investments. Get rid of a bad investment and replace it with a better selection.

Investors keep poor performers because they don't want to admit failure or they hope it will recover – thus the potential to profit from a better investment is lost.

Investors who routinely study *Value Line*® are better prepared to deal with these issues.

Learning the facts about potential stock selections strengthens confidence -- especially when a <u>written plan</u> is available to keep investors on the <u>right track</u>.

A positive attitude and accurate information are powerful investment resources that guide investors to create wealth -- investing whatever amount of money they can afford.

Long-term investors avoid trying to time the market seeking a dip in share value. Dollar-cost-averaging accomplishes the same long-term lower cost objective.

Long-term investments capture greater returns through price appreciation and the compounding of values. So what if the market crashes? Market dips are an opportunity to buy more shares at bargain prices!

Summary of Chapter 2 – Profitable Investing

- The reason to invest in stocks is to *create wealth*.

- Stocks are a safe and sure way to create wealth.

- The *Rules for Profitable Investing*© guide investors to plan, select, buy, and maximize the total return from investments.

- **Rules for Profitable Investing©**
    1. Have an investment plan
    2. Invest in growth companies
    3. Make your own decisions/exploit information
    4. Maximize *total return*
    5. Monitor/measure performance
    6. Adjust holdings -- if potential changes

- Because the stock market is in a <u>positive growth mode</u> most of the time, economic growth may fluctuate but always advances.

- *Have the right mindset.* Don't let myths or hype influence your decisions.

- Aim high -- for true potential!

- Manage your investments with current information, careful selection, and routine monitoring of performance.

Chapter 3

INVESTMENT PLAN ©

I/We _____, plan to invest $____ each month to routinely acquire shares of a growth company until 100 shares are owned before buying another company, and:

- The goal is to capture 17% <u>or more</u> in total return. Shares below this goal will be replaced.

- *Value Line®* will be reviewed before buying/selling.

- Share value will be maximized by buying company-direct, dollar-cost-averaging (DCA), re-investing dividends (DRIP), and holding long-term to exploit compounding.

- If money is needed in an emergency, a short-term margin loan will be considered rather than selling shares. Retained value of shares will grow in value faster than cost of a loan.

- Shares won't be sold in panic during downturns. If possible, extra shares will be bought at lower cost.

- Recording purchases, dividends, splits, sales, taxes, and fees will be kept up-to-date in an Investment Workbook.

- No one else is to manage or alter this plan.

Signed: _____ Date:_____

Copy this worksheet from the Appendix or downloaded from:
www.boddeneen.com/InvestmentPlan.htm

<u>Summary of Chapter 3 – Investment Plan</u>

- The focus of this book is on creating wealth from investing in growth and maximizing the total return.

- Investors that have written investment plans are more likely to be profitable investors.

- With research, study, and a plan, individuals can profitably manage their own investments -- especially when they <u>think positively</u>, <u>aim for maximum returns</u>, and continually <u>qualify investment performance</u>.

- Whereas expert strategies, and brokers, guide investors about buying and selling, managing their own investment portfolios assures investors that desired goals will be achieved.

- An *Investment Workbook* help investors stay on the right track to maximize the total return of investments. A plan and a workbook assure capturing what is aimed for.

Chapter 4

BUY & HOLD STRATEGY

During bull markets investors become careless. During bear markets they become excessively cautious. Neither response is favorable. Investors can create greater wealth when they adhere to proven strategies.

Although the goals of financial institutions are different from the goals of individual investors, each influence the general market --but in different ways.

Individual investors are the largest investor group, owning 80% of all stocks, but they trade less often and in smaller amounts than institutional investors. Individuals typically gain by holding investments long-term – thus capturing the benefits of compounding – the master builder of wealth.

Only by holding long-term can investors benefit from compounding! Compounding of value begins at about 15 years, then doubles, triples and quadruples in value in later years. It might take 50 years to reach $1 million, then only a few more years to reach $3 million. Institutional and day traders rarely experience this multiplication of value.

Tactics to create wealth are free and available to everyone. Strategies for profitable investing are well known. Successful investing depends on how well strategies are followed. For example *selection*.

Selection is a key element in buy & hold investing. *Careful selection* is vital when the amounts invested are small and potentially owned for many years. Because it is important the next chapter is dedicated selection.

When selected right, investments perform right. This does not mean that a carefully selected investment does not need watching. It means that buying a strong growth stock or fund will have the potential for low risk and high reward.

Maximizing total return is an objective every investor should aim for.

A good stock will have many years of <u>consistent growth</u>. Examples include GE, Pfizer, Proctor-Gamble, Coca-Cola, and many other established growth firms that are routinely reviewed in *Value Line*®.

Buying shares directly from the issuer lowers the cost of ownership. There are 1000 corporations that sell shares directly via dividend reinvestment programs (DRIPs). About 100 are desirable. Routine automatic deposits from personal bank accounts progressively builds ownership.

Shares beget shares!

Buying shares direct is a good habit that routinely adds value from splits that compound in value.

Buying through direct deposits requires an initial deposit that varies among corporations. Subsequent deposits accumulate as whole or fractional shares. Over time, fractional shares aggregate to full shares – thus shares beget shares.

When reinvested dividends accumulate as fractional or whole shares -- thus adding more shares to shareholder accounts. This potential is reviewed in a later chapter.

The remarkable rewards of direct deposits and long-term holdings become evident when a few dollars turn into thousands – and potentially millions – of dollars.

<u>Summary of Chapter 4 -- Buy & Hold Strategies</u>

- Successful investors create wealth by applying a few proven strategies.

- *Time* is more important than the amount of money invested.

- *Time* creates wealth via the steady accumulation of shares and the value-adding magic of compounding.

- By spending sufficient time to select the *right* stock, or mutual fund, investors enhance their ability to *maximize total return* -- even when investing little money.

- *The Rules for Profitable Investing©* provide the guidelines to excel as a buy & hold investor.

- With the right attitude and dedicated management, a few dollars will multiply to thousands -- and potentially millions of dollars.

Chapter 5

SELECTING THE RIGHT COMPANY

The goal of selection is to find stocks or mutual funds with greater than average long-term growth potential.

Buying on a whim -- without careful selection is a gamble and a major cause of mediocre gains or losses..

Regardless of how selected, replace mistakes quickly to prevent losing potential gain. Buying is a separate from selection – as reviewed in the next chapter.

Selecting the right *company*

All references to stocks, investments, or holdings include mutual funds and exchange traded funds (ETFs)..

Before buying, research at least three choices. First confirm an equity's *potential commercial growth*. Finding quality investments that excel in product and corporate management is not difficult -- *Value Line*® lists them.

Target annual stock market growth of at least the market average of 11% and higher. An achievable target is 15% growth, plus a 2% dividend, for a 17% total return.

The "company" to own is most important. You cannot manage the stock market, but you can manage the investment you own.

The best resource for selection is *Value Line Investment Surveys*® for unbiased information of 1700 stocks and the best 100. Whittle this list down by comparing *Value Line's* #1 stocks with *Standard & Poor*® ratings of "A".

In a perfect world stocks produce consistent growth. Although the investment world is not perfect, investors can improve their chances by seeking quality stocks. After selecting two or three, buy the one with the best potential.

There are ample long-term leaders. GE has been a quality investment for over 100 years. Exxon, Intel, AMD, or Microsoft may be the next leaders. Other examples are IBM, Coca-Cola, Johnson & Johnson, Procter-Gamble, Gillette, Pfizer, Dell, Wal-Mart, and Vanguard funds.

Note: Above are not recommendations – only research reveals the best.

Careful selection reduces the need for diversification -- which is a hedge against marginal performance. If investments are selected right diversity is less important. Diversity for the sake of diversity weakens the ability to maximize gains.

How can a small investor diversify when investment money is limited? For small investors, greater variety increases risk and lowers the potential for reward.

Two important aspects of selection are:
- ✓ **The company**
- ✓ **Performance**

What are the <u>strengths, weaknesses, opportunities, and threats of the company and its stock?</u> Before buying, compare two or three company stocks for:
- ✓ long-term growth potential
- ✓ control of *business* markets (% share?)
- ✓ highest possible *total* return
- ✓ potential risks

A stock may look good at first glance but if not carefully studied it could later turn sour. Selection is easier when you understand the company, its products, its market, and its potential growth.

Warren Buffett invests only in companies he understands. He researches financial data and judges business potential. He likes to invest in the things that people use daily.

Individual investors are not likely to explore as thoroughly as Buffet but every investor can explore:
- ✓ Potential for growth -- as rated by *Value Line*®
- ✓ Products -- innovations, sales, business market
- ✓ Management -- experience, performance, ethics
- ✓ Yield (dividend rate -- consistency of payment
- ✓ Timeliness & Safety -- as rated by *Value Line*®
- ✓ P/E Ratio
- ✓ Capital Rating

Evaluate strengths, weaknesses and threats in relation to the *Rules for Profitable Investing*© and summarize using the following *Selection Criteria* worksheet:

SELECTION CRITERIA®

Stock Symbol: _____ _____ _____

Growth Potential _____ _____ _____
Value Line rating -- 1 (best), 2 (good), 3 (marginal)

Products:
Sales growth _____ _____ _____
Marketshare _____ _____ _____
Innovations _____ _____ _____

Management
Experience _____ _____ _____
Performance _____ _____ _____
Ethics _____ _____ _____

Dividend
Payment consistency _____ _____ _____
DRIP -- Yes/No _____ _____ _____

Timeliness _____ _____ _____

Safety (*Value Line*) _____ _____ _____

P/E Ratio Price/EPS _____ _____ _____

Capital Rating _____ _____ _____

Notes:

What makes an investment desirable?

There are various opinions about what defines a desirable investment. Here are some factors:
- ✓ High *total* return -- growth & yield
- ✓ Extensive industry & management experience
- ✓ Excellent and innovative products/services
- ✓ Significant commercial marketshare
- ✓ Excellent management
- ✓ Desirable *Value Line* analysis and ratings

Favorable Return

Seek higher than average *percentage of return*. Between 1980 and 2000, the average annual return on major growth stocks was 20%. At the end of 2009, the Standard & Poor's 500-stock index gained 23.5% for the year.

According to the NY Times (1/20/2010): *After starting with a whimper, 2009 finished with a roar. What changed to ignite the turnaround? Nothing in the economy or corporate earnings. The main improvement was in people's moods and expectations.*

The emergence from the 2008 market gives investors the chance to acquire shares at lower cost. Saving even one-half percent in cost will multiply value over the long-term.

Consider GE's performance. $5,000 invested in 1978 grew to $38,000 by 1998. If $1,000 more had been invested in each of those 20 years ($20,000), $760,000 would have been earned! There is no guarantee this will ever repeat – but it could.

Extensive experience

With many years in a profitable business market, growth companies have the intrinsic value (cost vs. potential) to produce maximized returns. These companies can be studied in *Value Line*® performance reports that chart past and projected growth and analytically review management and business markets.

Excellent products/services

The primary reason companies are in business is *to get customers*. The second reason is to *be profitable*.

Unless a company has *a sufficient share* of its business market it is not a worthy investment. Stocks must have *business market strength*. In a mature commercial market three to five companies will share a market segment with one controlling 50% or more of that segment.

It will have taken ten to twenty years for that segment to mature and for the most successful firms to capture control. Unless a company controls at least a third of its marketshare why buy its stock? And don't let a popular make you complacent. IBM and Kodak stumbled after years of being business leaders.

If unable to make a selection compare the *Value Line*® summary with company's website summary of its market, products, and management.

Value of excellent business management

Even if you like a company, <u>assure that it is effective at marketing innovative products and services</u>.

There are hundreds of good products that lost marketshare because of weak marketing strategy – which happened to IBM, Kodak, Xerox and many others. Changes in management, ample resources, and other products helped most firms to recover.

Seek *Value Line*® ratings of "1 or 2" for *Timeliness*® and *Safety*®. Accept a *Timeliness of 1* and *Safety of 2* in a stable industry. The stock's analysis must be better than other choices. Or select only "1" ratings.

While reading about investments, make note of stocks that look promising. Subscribe online to the *Motley Fool* for unbiased investment advice. Eventually you will acquire investing competency and confidence.

As you research for potential selections eliminate superfluous information -- as with articles about bonds, foreign investments, day trading, or stock options.

As selection is the beginning to a long-term process there is no need to rush the process. The *right* selection strengthens the potential for high rewards while reducing risks.

<u>Summary of Chapter 5 -- Selecting the *Right* Stock</u>

- Selection is the process of *finding the right stock* to buy and hold long-term.

- Choose 2 or 3 stocks, then decide which <u>one</u> to buy.

- Haphazard selection increases risk and lowers the potential reward. Time and money are too precious to be wasted on hasty decisions.

- If selected right, a stock is less likely to later need replacement.

- Keep notes in your *Investment Workbook*:
    - ✓ *Selection Worksheet*©
    - ✓ <u>Potential for growth</u> -- as rated by *Value Line*™
    - ✓ Products, marketshare, management experience.
    - ✓ Dividend rate; consistency of payment; DRIP?
    - ✓ Timeliness & Safety -- as rated by *Value Line*™
    - ✓ P/E Ratio and Capital Rating
    - ✓ Aim for an annual return of 15% to 17%

- A "stock watch-list" is useful practice. It may take several weeks or months to create a suitable list but the gain in knowledge and confidence will last a lifetime of betterness investing.

Betterness At Investing

Chapter 6

BUYING THE RIGHT STOCK

After you find three potential winners, buy the stock with the best long-term *total return potential*. Buy as if it will be the only stock you will ever own. Accumulate 100 or more shares before making another investment.

Stocks can have desirable past records and mediocre futures. Between 1980 and 2000 IBM grew only 8% and Sears 9% while other growth firms averaged 20%. Although normally high growth companies, bad times in management and marketing made them temporarily undesirable for being below the ideal 17% in total return.

Plan for the best return by practicing the following:
- ✓ Buy growth
- ✓ Aim for at least a 17% <u>total</u> return
- ✓ Buy shares directly from the company
- ✓ Acquire shares consistently
- ✓ Reinvest dividends -- to acquire extra shares
- ✓ Hold long-term (20 years or more)
- ✓ Don't panic when the stock market declines
- ✓ Routinely monitor performance

Quality growth

Quality growth is the result of effective management and a strong commercial market position. Growth companies will have many years of profitable business from producing innovative products that attract and satisfy customers. They are the best or one of the best in their industry.

The combined performance of quality growth firms has created a 100-year record of stock values that average 11% annually. Individually, these firms produce total annual returns of 17% or better (15% plus 1.5% dividend).

Here are examples of 20-year average growth rates (minus dividends): Wal-Mart = 31%; Coca-Cola = 21%; Schering-Plough = 21%; GE = 20%; Merck = 20%; PepsiCo = 20%; Pfizer = 20%; Sara Lee = 19%; Disney = 18%; Johnson & Johnson =18%; McDonald's = 18%; Philip Morris =17%; Vanguard Energy = 16%.

Don't buy a stock based on recently high returns. Be sure the stock excels in all selection criteria. Nor sell it without first assuring it is no longer a good choice.

To accumulate shares at a lower average cost, make routine direct deposits into your shareholder account. A company's website will usually have an investor link that will explain the minimum amount required for a direct-deposit investor.

Direct deposits require being subscribed to the company's dividend reinvestment plan (DRIP). Deposits are credited each quarter and valued at the current market price.

Betterness At Investing

The need for stock *certificates* has ended. Anyone holding certificates can keep them until the stock is sold or transferred as a gift. Shareholder accounts and quarterly statements replace the need for certificates.

If making a gift of stock, the gift shares will be deducted from your account and transferred to the new owner. The new shareholder account will be opened after essential data (name, address, age, SS#) is provided to the transfer agent.

Gift shares are a great way to get children and grandchildren invested at an early age – possibly pay for college with the help of compounded value.

Summary of Chapter 6 -- Buying the Right Stock/Fund

- <u>Buy the stock of established growth companies.</u>

- Seek companies with years of business success, innovative products, excellent management, major control of business market, steady growth, a desirable dividend, and a DRIP.

- Seek a <u>minimum total return</u> of 17% (15% growth

- plus 1.5% to 2% in dividends).

- Buy stocks with a 1 or 2 *Value Line* ratings for *Timeliness* and *Safety*.

- Don't invest more than you can afford to routinely invest.

- Buy as if the only stock you will ever own.

- Accumulate at least 100 shares before acquiring another company.

- Sell poor performing stocks -- but only after checking *Value Line* projections of the stock and its possible replacement.

- Keep notes and records in an *Investment Workbook*.

- Use a watchlist to pre-sort selection choices.

Chapter 7

VALUE LINE INVESTMENT SURVEYS®

This chapter reviews a valuable resource for finding, selecting, and monitoring investments.

The author and publisher have no affiliation with *Value Line*®. This review has the approval of Value Line® for the benefit of investors.

Investment decisions require accurate information. Yet, in a national survey, a majority of investors said they *would like more information about investing*. They obviously did not know about *Value Line*®.

Warren Buffet, the most profitable stock investor, said: *Value Line is the best resource for investors; I don't know of any other system that's as good.*

Value Line® publishes data on 1700 active equities representing 94% of U.S. trading volume. Stocks are ranked relative to each other in price, performance, and risk every six to twelve months. Ratings for *Timeliness*© and *Safety*© are assigned to each stock.

Value Line *Timeliness*® ranked stocks outperform lower ranked stocks. *No other quantitative approach has proven more profitable.*

***Ratings & Reports*®** -- Part 3 of *Value Line*®
- ✓ Summaries of stock past/current performance,
- ✓ Industry review, and experienced analysis.
- ✓ Companies, by industry, assigned page
     number within their industry listing.
- ✓ Includes *Value Line's* proprietary ratings, defined
     for Timeliness and Safety:

Timeliness Rank -- 1© (Highest)
Expect the best, relative to performance during the next six to 12 months. Ranks of 100 stocks.

Timeliness Rank -- 2© (Above Average)
Better than average. Ranks 300 stocks.

Timeliness Rank -- 3© (Average)
Expect price performance in line with the market. Ranking of 3 is given to 900 stocks.

Safety Rank -- 1© (Highest)
One of the safest, most stable, and least risky.

Safety Rank -- 2© (Above Average)
Stock is safer, and less risky than most.

Safety Rank-- 3© (Average)
Average risk and safety ranking from 1 (high) to 5 (low). Goal: own stocks with ratings between 1 and 3.

Top row of company reports:
Company Name, Symbol, Recent Price ($), P/E Ratios,
Dividend Yield, Page/Reference Number

2nd Row:
- ✓ Timeliness, Safety, Beta ratings.
- ✓ Two year high/low projections for price & gain,
- ✓ Price Performance Graph + Projected path

Left Column
- ✓ Summary of company, Capital structure,
- ✓ Financial Position, Earnings per share, Dividends

Right/Bottom Section
- ✓ Business description (management, officers)
- ✓ Value Line's analysis:
- ✓ Financial Strength (A), Price Stability (90+),
  Growth Persistence (90+), Earnings Predictability

Weekly reviews summarize general market, as reported in:
- ✓ *Summary & Index*® -- **Part 1**
- ✓ *Selection & Opinion*® -- **Part 2**

Summary & Index -- **Part 1** -- ranking of 1700 companies.
Industries, in Order of Timeliness
Stocks prices, performance, safety, etc.
Small & Mid Cap with above average potential
Timely Stocks in Timely Industries
Stocks with highest performance in 12 months
High Yielding Stocks
Best Performing; Worst Performing
Highest Annual Total Return
Highest 3 to 5 Year Dividend

Selection & Opinion -- **Part 2**

The economy and stock market are reviewed each week with comparisons of data, market outlook, strategy, industry performance, performance highlights, and model portfolios:

The *Value Line View* -- Stock Highlights, Performance Record, Selected Investments, Selected Yields, Tracking the economy, and Market Monitor, Changes in Financial Strength Ratings, Closing Stock Averages.

As with anything worth doing, routine study will improve investor ability to select, buy, and manage investments. Each "Selection" section includes information for decisions, as with:

- ✓ Business Prospects
- ✓ Investment Advice, Closing Stock Market Averages
- ✓ Stock Highlights (list of 100 -- #1)
- ✓ Selected Investments -- 3 portfolios:
  - Portfolio I: Stocks for Performance
  - Portfolio II: Performance & Income
  - Portfolio III: Stocks for Long-term Growth
- ✓ Dow Jones Industrials: Earnings/Dividends
- ✓ Fixed Income Funds Average Performance
- ✓ Equity Funds Average Performance
- ✓ Growth Stocks with Low Risk
- ✓ Market Monitor (Industry Performance)
- ✓ Market Averages

The magnitude of this information may at first overwhelm novice investors, but it becomes clear with experience. Only by actual study can the full value of *Value Line®* be appreciated as with **Desirable ratings:**

- ✓ Beta (volatility rating)   1
- ✓ *Timeliness & Safety*   1
- ✓ Company's Financial Strength   A or B++
- ✓ Price Growth Persistence   100
- Earnings Predictability   100

Data that will not be up-to-date in *Value Line* reports are current prices. However, investors reviewing *Value Line* in libraries, can find current share prices listed in newspapers – local newspapers Wall Street Journal, and online listings.

Research is an essential task that is improved with accurate, useful, and easy-to-understand information -- as consistently provided in *Value Line Investment Surveys®*.

> ***Value Line is the next best thing***
> ***to having your own private securities analyst.***
> — Peter Lynch, *One Up on Wall Street*

Summary of Chapter 7: *Value Line* ®

- Having accurate, timely, and precise data conveniently listed in one reference is a valuable tool for every investor.

- *Value Line*® publishes sufficient data to make intelligent *selection*, *buying*, and *selling decisions*.

- Investors should never buy or sell a stock without first reviewing *Value Line*®.

- Stocks rated #1 by *Value Line*® have traditionally exceeded the average performance of other indexes.

- To make a right selection consider *Value Line*® *for:*
    - ✓ Listings of 10 years of Profitable growth.
    - ✓ Timeliness & Safety ratings
    - ✓ Dividend yield
    - ✓ History of steady dividends
    - ✓ Effective management
    - ✓ Profitable business market position
    - ✓ Financial rating of "A"

- Buying stocks rated #1 or #2 -- for Timeliness® & Safety® simplifies selection and buying.

Betterness At Investing

Chapter 8

<u>Mutual Funds</u>

Funds are desirable for investors who do not have the time or interest to research, select, and buy shares of stock. Funds are not risk free but many have been routinely profitable.

Funds seem to be useful for investors who:
- ✓ are not confident, or too busy, to make selections.
- ✓ are willing to pay a fee for this service.
- ✓ do not mind relinquishing ownership control.
- ✓ seek better returns than what they might achieve.

Funds have been useful for people unable to spend time managing their own portfolio. <u>Unfortunately some funds may have higher costs than do-it-yourself investing</u> when buy-in (load) and management fees are added to their cost. And, investors can be subjected to capital gains tax without receiving cash.

A fund's 3 to 5 year performance record is as important as its current year's performance. As with stocks, a profitable past does not assure profitable future growth.

Each year a fund's capital gains are reported to the IRS – which occurs <u>without cash distribution</u>. Each shareholder is allocated their share of this tax that is reported before the end of the year and therefore impacts on investor's current tax year.

<u>Asset Value</u> (NAV)
Fund shareholders own shares in the fund and not in the invested companies. The value of all of the shares, less expenses, determines the fund's NAV.

A survey by the *Association of Individual Investors* (AII) revealed that individual investors average higher annual returns than fund investors because of the cost of fees -- yet, several funds have higher returns than what most individual investors achieve.

Several mutual funds have low fees and high returns. Vanguard has some of the highest returns (35 to 70%), and lowest management fees (0.25).

Daily newspapers, investment magazines, and *Value Line* list and compare funds. Some broker accounts sell funds and offer advice. Decide which fund to buy based on its record of profits and fees.

Do not buy any fund that requires a buying fee known as a front-end load.

As with stocks, practice makes perfect. Create a virtual portfolio to monitor your pretend selections for a few weeks or months.

Mutual funds give investors the opportunity to broaden areas of interest; for example, to diversify or to invest in global emerging markets.

Because of their popularity, there are almost as many mutual funds as stocks. Funds are supposedly better than what an individual might accomplish but all funds do not fulfill that objective. Fund managers can make poor decisions and fees can be expensive. The potential benefits continue to make funds a valuable option as with the returns for two of Vanguard's best funds:

Vanguard Funds – Year End, 2009

	1 yr	**3 yr**
Emerging Markets (VEIEX)	74.67%	14.37%
Energy (VGENX)	38.36	13.38%

Imagine owning these funds at a time when many people considered that it was a poor time to invest!

Summary of Chapter 8 -- Mutual Funds

- Mutual Funds can be profitable for some investors, but fees make funds costlier than individually owned stock.

- Investors who do not have the time, or desire, to research, select, and buy shares of stock can benefit from investing in mutual funds.

- The professional management of funds can be an asset – especially with a record of profitability.

- Investors have no input in a fund's transactions or in maximizing total return. Profits remain in the fund, but shareholders must pay their share of a fund's capital gains accrued from share turnover (trading).

- There are 6000 funds. If not confident to manage your investments, consider an equity fund that paces the market -- such as *Vanguard Index Fund* or *TIA-CREFF* -- which have decent results and low management fees.

- Worth Magazine annually rates *The Top 20 Mutual Fund Companies* for equity and bond funds.

- As with stocks, list funds of interest in your virtual (practice) portfolio.

Chapter 9

EXCHANGE TRADED FUNDS

Because mutual funds lacked the flexibility of owning stock, *Exchange Traded Funds* (ETFs) were created to trade the same as shares stock – and with tax benefits.

Initially designed to enable investors to own a "package" of stocks listed on an index (S&P 500, etc.) additional packages were added to include global markets, known as Emerging Market ETFs.

As emerging markets were in reality developed markets, iShares were introduced to target specific countries, such as Brazil and other small but growing markets.

While a bit confusing to beginning investors, ETF give investors wanting the professional management of funds the ability to trade as they would shares of stock.

Because ETFs do not turn-over (sold) as often as mutual funds the tax consequences are less than with standard funds that declare gains without distributing cash to investors. Thus, standard funds have unique tax consequences.

Because of their robust growth, emerging markets have been a profitable investment – whether in a standard fund or ETF. As there is always greater risk with greater reward, emerging markets are a more volatile investment. Losses can be as great as the gains – yet investors who stay the course generally profit as markets tend to recover and grow higher.

More about ETFs

An index is a collection of securities in a specific market. Holdings within the index are constituents. Size of an index varies. The Russell 3000 Index has 3000 constituents. An index for a single country or industry may have only 30 constituents.

ETFs can be traded throughout a trading day and bought on margin, sold short, or traded as a limit order.

Each index has its own goals. Index-based investing offers lower costs than traditional funds. Risk is reduced as index funds are highly diversified with several securities.

ETFs are beneficial for investors who buy/hold, dollar-cost-average (DCA), make routine deposits (DRiP), and seek reasonable fees.

Investors might start with the fund that launched ETFs: *Vanguard pioneered mutual fund indexing a generation ago, and today, Vanguard ETFs take advantage of Vanguard's experience.*

Vanguard ETFs give you the opportunity to enjoy the benefits of indexing — a diverse investment strategy, low operating costs, and the potential for high tax-efficiency.

More about iShares:

While offering a greater selection, with over 195 ETFs in every possible market – financial and industrial, domestic and global – iShares tend to cost more to own (*higher expense ratio*). However, they offer investors the ability to target countries, especially the popular "BRICs" (Brazil, Russia, India, China). Single country investments may not offer small dollar investors the security of broad emerging market ETFs.

Emerging Markets

Besides emerging markets, ETFs are offered in numerous markets – financial, mid-cap, large-cap, growth, etc, etc – to view Vanguard's listing go to:

https://personal.vanguard.com/funds/reports/total_return_chart.pdf?cbdForceDomain=true

Practice List

As ETFs are complex, and volatile, novice investors can practice with a virtual portfolio and track online until sufficiently confident to make a real-time investment.

Summary of Chapter 9 -- Exchange Traded Funds

- ETFs are a practical solution for investors wanting diverse mutual fund holdings in many markets – with benefits similar to stock shares.

- Several global markets that have a greater rate of growth than the U.S. market offer investors huge profit opportunities – thus ETFs for emerging markets have become very popular.

- Because ETFs are unique and more complex than common stocks, novice investors, would be wise to have a practice portfolio to track until they are confident of the risks and rewards of ETFs.

രു✧ൽ

Betterness At Investing

Chapter 10

MAXIMIZING TOTAL RETURN

With a few easy-to-apply, no-cost tactics, investors can squeeze extra profits from corporate stock holdings.

Assertive attention determines whether a portfolio grows to thousands, hundreds of thousands, or millions of dollars. Why yearn for high returns when you can create them?

Investors who apply value-adding tactics are rewarded with the compounding of investment value. Tactics that capture higher gains include:

- ✓ Aiming for a high total return (*seek & find*)
- ✓ Accumulating as many shares as possible
- ✓ Buying at lower average cost
- ✓ Buying direct from a company
- ✓ Reinvesting dividends
- ✓ Routinely investing each month or quarter

Tactics to maximize profits are free to every investor. Investors who think negatively about this potential are not likely to seek higher returns. Investors who do not doubt their ability to capture higher returns earn higher returns.

Every cost savings, DRIP gain, and compounding, create wealth. The following reveals how higher return can multiply into substantial long-term gains.

Rule of 72

To estimate when investments will double in value <u>divide 72 by the percentage of return</u>. The following double in 6.5 years @ 11% annual return and 4.2 years @ 17%.

$1,000 @ 11% annual return – year end of total gain:

Year 7	Year 14	Year 21	Year 28
$2,016	$4,310	$8,949	$18,578

$1,000 @17% annual return:

Year 5	Year 9	Year 14	Year 19	Year 24
$2,192	$4,108	$9,007	$19,748	$43,297

(Note: Estimates of gross profits before fees and taxes)

These examples demonstrate what is possible, but not guaranteed. For example, it shows how an extra 6% speeds up value by doubling 35% faster. More is gained in 19 years @17% -- than in 28 years @ 11%.

Start with $25 a month; in 3.5 years it will grow to $1,000. Imagine adding deposits each year! Profitable investors <u>apply all factors that maximize profits</u>, as with:

- ✓ Dollar Cost Averaging -- routinely buying to acquire shares at a lower <u>average cost</u>.
- ✓ Buying shares direct from company.
- ✓ Dividend Reinvestment (DRIPs).
- ✓ Welcome stock splits – more shares at no cost.

Betterness At Investing

Dollar Cost Averaging (DCA)
Average share cost will be less when buying at a fixed cost on a fixed schedule, regardless of the equity's price. DCA is well established for averaging lower in cost than when holding back to make a lump sum deposit. The price you hope to buy at may not repeat.

Buying shares direct from a company:
About 1000 companies sell shares direct to individuals. Most are commission-free; some have a small fee. Amounts accepted for monthly deposit range from $10 to $10,000. Deposits are reported quarterly. Links to direct investing are listed in the Appendix.

As buying direct saves money, more shares can be acquired. A shareholder's account is credited for whole or fractional shares.

If share price is $50 and $25 is deposited, the account is credited with .50 (1/2) share. Some require initial investments of $100 to $250. Enrollment in a DRIP may be mandatory.

Dividend Reinvestment Plan (DRIP)
The lower dividend tax increased investor desire to own stocks that share (yield) earnings. In a DRIP account, dividends are paid in cash or shares. Dividends paid in shares beget more shares with each subsequent reinvestment. In a DRIP, dividends are paid in shares credited as whole or fractional value equal to the dollar amount of the dividend.

Stock Splits

Companies split shares to maintain an attractive share price with a lower investment cost. Shares may be split in many ratios, but typically are two for one (2:1). Share prices typically appreciate in value after a split and eventually rebound to the prior value.

A 2:1 split does not immediately increase portfolio value but usually will increase beyond the price prior to the split – but will accumulatively increase the value of holdings.

Corporate directors declare a split when they believe share price is too high to attract investors. A $50/share, split 2:1 creates two $25 shares. Initially, total value will be the same but a lower share price tends to drive the price back up to its prior value.

Between 1978 and 1998 a share of GE grew to 16 shares as the result of splits. 100 shares became 1600 shares by 1998. In 1978 the price was $51 and in 1998, $74 per share. Thus 100 shares originally valued at $5,100 grew to $118,400.

Paper Profit

The number of shares owned can be more important than their current value. Future value may grow 20 or 30 times greater. However, until shares are sold, current value is simply paper profit.

There is no guarantee of future value. Investors are always at risk of price reduction. However when share prices fall the number of shares does not change. If you don't sell no cash is lost.

Exploit Compounding of value

Time and the *compounding of value* create wealth.

A single investment of $1,000 returning 17% annually can grow (via compounding) to $1 million in 44 years.

Investing $1,000 a year ($1,000 x 40 = $40,000) could produce $3.3 Million in 40 years. Think about it!

Respect dividend yields! A 5% annual dividend adds 25% in five years, and 50% in ten years. Even a 2% yield maximizes the value of holdings.

Caution, these are theoretical calculations. They demonstrate how investments might *maximize*.

Believe in your potential to create wealth:

During the 90s, long-term investments in quality growth firms averaged 25% annually. At the same time conservative experts were saying that 12% was the average return investors could expect -- based on the total market. Thus, investors who ignored the experts and applied value-adding tactics to *carefully selected growth companies* had better returns.

Summary of Chapter 10 -- Maximizing Total Return

- Wealth is created long-term by capturing lower costs per share, accumulating as many shares as possible, and allowing compounding to maximize portfolio value.

- Several options to maximize value are freely available to every investor:
  - ✓ Direct commission-free purchases
  - ✓ Dollar-cost-averaging (DCA)
  - ✓ Dividend Reinvest Plan (DRIP)
  - ✓ Stock splits
  - ✓ Holding long-term for compounding to kick in

- Routine fixed monthly or quarterly deposits acquire shares at lower average cost.

- *Buy & Hold* does not mean buy & forget! Routinely monitor and measure performance.

- Stay calm during market crashes. Accumulate shares at a lower cost per share.

- Follow the *Rules For Profitable Investing*.

- So what if results are less than targeted? So what if you gain $800,000 instead of $1 million? Why settle with $400,000 when $800,000 could have been achieved?

Chapter 11

PORTFOLIO MANAGEMENT

Indifference is a threat to profitable investing. Investors cannot afford to buy & forget. Lack of attention to performance and total return can invite losses or miss out on capturing extra gains.

Routine review is essential to assure accuracy of data and fulfillment of goals. Complacent and inconsistent action causes investors to:

✓ Buy and sell without researching *Value Line®*.
✓ Abandon routine investment deposits.
✓ Seek quick profits.
✓ Fail to exploit all options to maximize growth.
✓ Fail to replace stocks that have turned sour.
✓ Panic when the market crashes.

Stocks bought or sold with *fear*, *greed*, or *impatience* expose investors to greater risks. Bad decisions mess up investment portfolios.

Make no decision without *facts* and *objectives*. Make no decision without a full analysis. Review *Value Line®*. Stay focused on the investment plan. Base decisions on facts, not fears.

Managing Gains

Long-term holdings can make investors eager to turn profits into cash. If cash is desired it is better to sell only a small portion. James O'Neill of *Investors Business Daily* suggests taking some cash when gains exceed 20 percent of portfolio value.

Lingering Safety

There is safety in time. When measuring *S&P 500* stocks, Ibbotson Associates discovered that *the chance of loss is only 3% after holding for 10 years.* From Value Line's experience, *no investment has lost money when held over twenty years.*

There will always be worriers. Forbes columnist Ken Fisher described *fear of heights (acrophobia) as an investment disease. Bull markets climb a wall of worry.*

Fisher sited a major investment publication that was bearish in 1995 -- and at the end of the year the Dow was up 36 percent!

Although market downturns are temporary, investors must prepare for whatever length of time it takes for a recovery. Money is not lost if no stocks are sold. When the market is depressed investors can acquire shares at bargain prices.

Record keeping

The worksheets on the following pages are tools to help investors with portfolio management.

PORTFOLIO SUMMARY ©

Quarterly Review: Date_____

Company:	# Shs	$ Cost	Total Value	$ Gain	% Gain
Yield ___%					
_____	__	__	__	__	__
_____	__	__	__	__	__
_____	__	__	__	__	__
_____	__	__	__	__	__
_____	__	__	__	__	__
TOTAL	__	__	__	__	__	__
# Shares	__	__	__	__	__	__
Aver. $/ Sh	__	__	__	__	__	__

Summary for Year: _____

Quarter	Total Value	#Shares	Gain(Loss)	
_____	$_____	_____	$_____	_____%
_____	$_____	_____	$_____	_____%
_____	$_____	_____	$_____	_____%
_____	$_____	_____	$_____	_____%
Year-end:	$_____	_____	$_____	_____%

Notes:

_____

_____

Betterness At Investing

Investment Workbook

Workbooks help investors organize information accurately. A 3-ring binder or a computer file are useful for storing:

☞ **Investment Plan** -- keep the plan available for routine review and to monitor performance.

☞ **Transactions** -- keep a record of transactions, dividends, and stock splits. Save shareholder quarterly statements.

☞ **Selection Notes** -- keep copies of *Value Line* summaries of stocks to watch and stock bought. Save related notations for portfolio updates.

☞ **Quarterly Statements** -- shareholders of record receive a corporate statement of their holdings each quarter. These statements confirm purchases and sales that provide data for accounting and tax reporting.

☞ **Form 1099 Statements** -- each year investors receive an IRS Form 1099 reporting dividends paid in cash or stock. This is the same form used for interest-bearing accounts.

☞ **Performance Reviews** -- store projections and actual performance. Measure gains in percentages.

☞ **Practice Portfolio** -- an imaginary watch-list is a useful way to decide what to own. Pretend to own each stock on list and track performance.

Investment Clubs

Investment clubs help investors. Clubs trade as a group and members share equally in the group's portfolio. The club's portfolio need not match a personal portfolio. *The National Association of Investment Clubs®* (NAIC) provides kits to organize and manage clubs.

Financial Planning Assistance

Most investors can manage small portfolios but need help with larger portfolios. They also need help with tax issues, which requires the assistance of a CPA or CFA.

A CPA or Certified Financial Advisor (CFA) or Planner (CFA/P) can help with investments and taxes. CPAs are CFAs are licensed and sell only services. Be wary of "advisors" who sell products.

More About Brokers

Brokers may be useful but personal control is needed. In a 1996 Buffalo News article, Jane Bryant Quinn revealed that *brokers mishandle customer accounts, sell inappropriate investments, and persuade you to trade excessively. Brokers like this don't exist in a vacuum. Their bosses ignore bad track records and have misled honest brokers.*

In 2003, the NY State Attorney General took several brokers to court. The guilty verdict resulted in large fines. Be a do-it-yourself investor -- never give anyone control of your investments.

Good brokers exist -- ask friends to recommend one.

Settling With Uncle Sam

Annual dividends are reported to investors and the IRS via Form 1099 (non-employee income). Dividends are reported in the year received whether or not reinvested.

No tax is due on capital gains until shares are sold. The exception is mutual funds; investors pay capital gains on annual trades, known as fund turnover.

The difference between the cost (purchase price plus fee) and selling price (income minus fees) is the gain. If you expect large gains consult a CPA to determine the tax impact. But don't hold on to a poor-performing stock to avoid a tax.

Staying informed

Review *Value Line Reports & Summaries®* once a month as a new investor and each quarter when experienced. Scan investment magazines for stocks to compare with *Value Line's* #1 rated companies. *Value Line®* may offer a low cost Library Patron's Discount for a 6-month trial subscription. Call 800/535-9648 or check online at their website (see Appendix).

Research Facts:

Portfolio management depends on details. Never invest without accurate data. Never buy/sell without researching *Value Line®*.

Disciplined Patience

Impatience can interfere with effective portfolio management. Holding investments for 20 to 40 years requires disciplined trust.

It's not always possible to stay calm during a market crash, but taking no action is often the best strategy. Selling can create losses (no sale; no loss). When in doubt, review the future value that compounding will produce.

Routinely measure *percentage*

Measure gains (or losses) as a *percentage*. Most investors know the dollar value of gains (or losses), but few know the percentage. Percentages qualify performance. A $5,000 gain sounds good, but if in a $100,000 portfolio it is only a 5% gain!

However, respect all gains. A 5% extra return (17% vs. 12%) doubles the amount gained in 15 years! This rate of doubling does not at first appear great but long-term it is significant. Using spreadsheets, investors can compare how an extra 5% can produce a five times greater return.

Effective portfolio management assures that plans are fulfilled, mistakes avoided or quickly corrected, and that the full potential total return is captured.

The most profitable investors patiently manage the performance of their investments.

Summary of Chapter 11 -- Portfolio Management

- How a portfolio performs is determined by how well it's managed.

- Buy & Hold does not mean Buy & Forget.

- *Portfolio Summaries©* and *Investment Workbooks©* help investors manage more effectively.

- *Value Line®* is the single best investor reference.

- Ignore market and media hype. Concentrate on the essential details quality growth companies.

- Be consistent, disciplined, and patient. Follow the *Rules for Profitable Investing©*. Let *time* and *compounding* create wealth.

- If a beginning investor, create a practice portfolio to put the strategies from this book into practice before buying stock.

- Investors must control the performance of their portfolio by making their own decisions. How well a portfolio performs is under the control of its owner.

Betterness At Investing

Chapter 12

TEACH INVESTING TO YOUNGSTERS

Learning how to put money to work – to earn more money – is a priceless lifetime lesson. Youngsters learn the value of time, how small but consistent deposits can grow to great value, and how the magic of compounding multiplies that value. They also learn the rewards of good management.

This lesson is so important the government is providing schools with lesson plans to introduce students to financial management.

Because teenagers are usually inquisitive, and have time to study and manage investments, they can become profitable investors. As owners of cars, computers, and other equipment -- earned from work and gifts – teenagers are affluent consumers who can afford to make small initial investments.

Youngsters need to know that a single investment of $1,000 – as from an inheritance – can grow to $1 million within fifty years. And, that routine small deposits can accomplish the same thing – all from the magic of compounding.

Teenagers need to learn how to use money wisely. The Bible tells a story of a cautious servant who was punished for not investing money entrusted to him. He let it sit idle -- producing no gain. By learning about investing, teenagers become better providers, employees, executives, and citizens.

Youngsters who learn to invest also learn about American enterprise. Creating a profitable portfolio will give young people the freedom to work at what they enjoy and the ability to retire at an earlier than typical age.

Children grasp the excitement of stock ownership. Evidence of this was seen on ABC TV (8/01/1995). A financial advisor and his children were being interviewed on *Good Morning America*. The father started his children investing at a young age. They learned to buy & hold shares and reinvest dividends.

The daughter said her father taught her *not to panic if the market crashed as long-term growth was more important.* She was fifteen. Her younger brother, held shares in Telefono de Mexico, which *went south* in value, but he kept buying in order to accumulate shares at a lower average cost.

Unless young people receive effective guidance they are likely to grow up with flawed understanding of investing. This is evident by the questions newspapers and magazines receive from adults. An online resource -- *The Motley Fool®* -- is fun and educational.

An Abundant Future
If an investment of $1,000 can become $50,000 in 25 years and $1 million in 50 years, imagine what teenagers can accomplish! They could become middle-aged millionaires; perhaps billionaires if extra money is invested.

Teenagers make decisions about money everyday. They are knowledgeable consumers. For this reason alone, they need to learn how to use their money as a resource for wealth creation. Unfortunately, what teenagers hear or read is too often negative. They need to know the positive facts.

A Lifetime of Benefits
Don't wait until kids are older to give gifts of stock. They are likely to grow up thinking there is plenty of time to learn about investing. Why wait? Investment accounts can be opened with an adult co-owner. Kids will learn to manage investment paperwork and records.

<u>Summary of Chapter 12 – Teaching Youngsters</u>

- Teenagers have discretionary *money* and *time* to become successful investors.

- With a little startup money and guidance they can create wealthy portfolios.

- Relatives who want to help should:
  - ✓ Include teenagers in investment discussions
  - ✓ Give gifts of stock
  - ✓ Encourage and show kids how to invest
  - ✓ Share this book with them
  - ✓ Review the "*Rules of Investing*" with them
  - ✓ Open a joint bank investment account

- Encourage teenagers to join an investment club -- or help them start one in school or at home.

- Show them how to create a practice portfolios applying the *Rules of Investing©* and information from *Value Line®*.

- Helping teenagers invest prepares them for a lifetime of better living. They learn the value of time, the magic of compounding -- as with how time and a little money create wealth.

- The have the *time* to become millionaires -- perhaps billionaires -- before they retire.

Chapter 13

SHARING WEALTH

Everything we have is on loan to us from God. What we do with our wealth is an important part of life. After providing for self and family, help others.

As a nation we spend more on entertainment and gambling than we do to help fellow citizens. More money is spent breeding race horses than on feeding hungry people!

Consider helping your church, synagogue, temple -- which are organized to help various needs. Consider giving directly to useful agencies, such as *Habitant for Humanity*, *Mercy Ships*, *Salvation Army*, food kitchens and shelters.

Think of how you could help with donations of cash or stock to so many worthy causes. Start a fund with $1,000, $10,000, or $100,000 invested in quality growth stocks. Appoint yourself as the trustee to manage the fund until a goal is reached. Motivate others to follow your example. Invite them to invest in your fund. Work together to achieve greater gifting potential.

So what if it takes 15 years before distribution begins? If enough people donated 2% of their profits there would be ample support for all worthy needs.

The ideal fund has a plan that defines how objectives and goals are to be fulfilled. Annual distributions would be controlled to preserve the fund size.

Private support could replace programs that have been reduced or dropped by cuts in government spending.

A few agencies deal with copious needs. *Mercy Ships* delivers medical care to health-poor countries. The *Salvation Army* helps anyone in need. Local agencies care for the homeless and hungry. *Habitat for Humanity* builds affordable homes. Religious groups, the *Red Cross* and *United Way* fill a variety of emergency and economic needs.

Why wait for estate gifting? Start a fund now that will grow exponentially from compounding. If you are young enough (25, 40, 60, 70) you will be able to create substantial funding. Investing money to later be donated assures that every dollar creates more dollars. A <u>dollar multiplied by compounding</u> helps whole lot more than a dollar immediately spent.

If you don't have enough money or extra stock to start a fund, ask friends and relatives to join with you to create a fund. A few people with a little money can help a lot of needy people -- if invested right.

Ten donations of $1,000 would create a $10,000 fund and $10,000 gifts would create a $100,000 fund. Potentially these trusts would grow in value to $100,000 and $1 million (or more) in fifteen to twenty years when values compound.

Check with local funding agencies. Find out which projects need help. Or have them manage your fund.

If you can afford to donate cash that would be generous. However, convince agencies that for every dollar maximized by compounding they will have 20 to 30 times more from your fund than from a current gift.

Your invested gifts will keep on giving beyond your lifetime.

- Whatever we have is on loan to us from God. How it is used is as important as how we live.

- Create a funding portfolio for charitable giving.

- Control cash disbursements to assure continual growth. Protect the principal by limiting pay out.

- Hold disbursements until compounding kicks in or until the desired value is achieved, whether $100,000 or $1 million.

- So what if it takes 15 to 20 years to reach the pay out goal. Time to create wealth goes by quickly -- and positively.

- Imagine if funds had been started 15 years ago. Imagine what could be accomplished with the tens of thousands or hundreds of thousands of dollars that would now be available for useful purposes!

- Imagine your donations being continually useful.

Chapter 14

COMPOUNDING REVISITED

Many investors don't appreciate the potential of compounding. If they did, there would be more long-term investors.

Elements that make <u>long-term stock investing more productive</u> than other methods are *time* and *compounding*.

<u>Given sufficient time, compounding multiplies profits</u>. With more time, more profits. The best way to illustrate this wonderful benefit is to show examples.

The following examples are based on two average annual returns. One is the 100 year annual average of 11% and one a ten year average of 15% (1983-2003) -- plus a 2% average yield -- for a total return of 17%.

Examples are not adjusted for price swings as they average out over time to equal typical results. The <u>potential</u> for higher gains is more important than the exact final amount.

No aim, no gain. Investors exceed normal returns by owning growth stocks and aiming for maximum returns. Notice what happens when sufficient time is given for values to compound.

$1, 000 investment @ 11% annual return:

End of Year	Gain	Total Value
1	$ 110	$ 1,110
2	$ 122	$ 1,232
3	$ 135	$ 1,368
4	$ 150	$ 1,518
5	$ 167	$ 1,685
10	$ 281	**$ 2,839**
20	$ 799	**$ 8,062**
25	$ 1,346	**$ 13,585**

Notice that gains *accelerated* at years 10, 20, and 25! Imagine if a higher return had been captured!

$1, 000 invested @ 17% annual return:

Year	Gain	Total Value	
1	$ 170	$ 1,170	
5	$ 319	$ 2,192	
10	**$ 698**	**$ 4,807**	$ 2,000 more
15	**$ 1,531**	**$ 10,539**	$ 5,700 more!
20	**$ 3,357**	**$ 23,106**	$15,000 more!
25	**$ 7,361**	**$ 50,658**	**$37,000 more!**

Why settle for $13,585 when for the same investment -- at no additional cost -- you can earn $50,658?

Imagine if $5,000, $10,000, or $20,000 had been added routinely to capture four to five times greater gains!

Researching *Value Line* and resolving not to accept mediocre returns investors can find quality growth stocks.

Time is a more valuable investor resource than money. Time multiplies value through compounding. A 2003 article in the Buffalo News reiterated that *time adds value at an increasing rate, turning inept investors into winners. With enough time you don't need a large amount of capital to start out with.*

For Congress's Consideration
As time and compounding enable long-term investments to multiply in value <u>why not fund *Social Security* with long-term investments</u>?

A large initial investment is not required, and as *Social Security* is already a long-term scheme, Wouldn't it be wise to fund it from our country's economic growth?

Investments in a secure index fund of quality growth firms would be safe and profitable. Returns would equal or excel the 100 year 11% average. Dividends could add and average of 2% more. And, be safe form political control.

Investments could be placed in the S&P 500 or in a new index of the top 100 growth firms listed in Value Line's #1 rated stocks.

If the federal government invested $500 for every new citizen, by the age 65 that citizen would have $442,000 - - based on the 11% annual average.

Additional personal deposits could increase the value to $1 million and more.

Even without additional deposits a higher return is possible with higher annual average returns of 15% or more – thus potentially increasing the value to $2 or $3 million.

Current SS monthly payouts average $1,000 a month, which over time pays recipients $200,000 to $400,000. As citizens are living longer these payments could double in a few years. However, with stock investments the governments share would never exceed $500! And that could be repaid with the first withdrawal.

Workers and employers already contribute to SS -- in taxes to the Treasury. If the government invested in this country's economy, SS taxes could be reduced, perhaps eliminated, with all citizens fully invested in a private secure stock fund.

Politicians would not be able to tap into these funds unlike current SS funds. The government's $500 initial deposit could be repaid with interest at a higher than the Federal Reserve rate.

Savings in current spending would enable the government to be more charitable about social, health, educational and environmental issues. Income could be taxed at lower rates.

Irrational fears are a major obstacle to solving SS. Myths get more attention than facts. These concerns could be overcome with education and a citizen's advisory board.

It's ironic that a country with robust economic growth, the government does not share in that growth -- but grabs income by taxation. SS investments would foster greater growth from compounding of profits!

Our government lacks the courage to face this threat as an opportunity to solve a national problem. When the enormous potential of *time* and *compounding* is understood, long-term investments must be respected. Why shouldn't the government directly share in this wealth?

Disbursements could begin before age 65. At age 60 a small share of an individual's account might be withdrawn to enable citizens to reinvest or buy whatever they wanted. These distributions would continually boost the economy.

Summary of Chapter 14 -- Compounding Revisited

- Compounding makes <u>long-term investing</u> more productive than any other investment.

- Wealth can be created with *little money and lots of time.* However fear, doubt, and impatience keep people from enjoying the benefit of compounding.

- The issue of Social Security running short of money could be solved with a secure index fund -- with initial government deposits of $500, plus optional personal deposits. SS invested funds could have values $400,000 to millions of dollars for individual citizens. The government would be reimbursed its initial investment.

- There is over 100 years of proof that stocks are safe and sure investments.

- Until *compounding* is understood and respected, people and the government will continue to ignore this fantastic potential.

CHAPTER 15

MISCELLANEOUS INVESTING TOPICS

This chapter reviews things less essential to new investors but are topics that experienced investors will want to know about, as with:
- ✓ Asset Allocation
- ✓ Asset Management
- ✓ Trusts
- ✓ More about bonds
- ✓ Beating the Market
- ✓ Expert advice
- ✓ Foreign Investments
- ✓ Fundamental vs. Technical Analysis
- ✓ Can 1929 be repeated?
- ✓ Market Indices
- ✓ Stock Exchanges
- ✓ Corporate and Brokerage crime
- ✓ The Economy

Asset Allocation

Stocks, bonds, cash may be spread around to balance risk. A 50/40/10 allocation has 50% in stocks, 40% in bonds, and 10% in cash. Long-term investors often fully invest in stocks until retirement, then allocations may be 50/50 or 40/60 in stocks & bonds.

Asset Managed Accounts

Financial firms are assigned management of client investments with authority to sell/buy equities. Control may require owner approval and the requirement to fulfill special instructions as in a trust. Managed accounts are used for orphaned children, widows, or ailing patients. Although conservatively invested they are subject to market volatility. Since do-it-yourself investing has become popular and profitable, more heirs are capable of managing assets free of expensive management fees.

Trusts

Trusts are legal documents created to define how assets are to be managed after death or disability. Every asset (property, bank accounts, investment) must be transferred to the trust (e.g. Your Name Trust). The person creating the trust is the primary trustee. Trusts protect assets from probate, but may not avoid state taxes.

More about Bonds

Bonds are safe investments but have a different makeup than stocks. Bonds provide asset protection and fixed income. Issuers can recall *callable bonds* when interest rates fall.

Corporate bonds raise money for projects to build factories, college dormitories, roads, Whereas T-bonds raise money for the Treasury, municipal and prisons.

Face value ranges from $1,000 and higher. Annual interest -- typically 3% to 7% -- is paid at intervals. Monthly for higher value bonds ($10,000 +) and semiannually for lower value ($1,000 - $5,000) bonds. Retirees can buy in amounts to establish a desired monthly or quarterly income.

The *effective return* on bonds will be greater than the declared rate if *purchased at discount (sold at premium)*. A bond's face value is repaid at maturity in ten, twenty or thirty years. A 6%, $1,000 bond purchased at 15% discount costs $850. The *effective return* (due to the discount) would be 7.64%.

Beating the Market
Investors often beat the market with large one-time investments. One scheme, *Beat-the-Dow,* requires investing $10,000 in the ten "Dogs of the Dow" -- the lowest performers at year-end.

Surprisingly the "dogs" usually rebound in the succeeding year and investors "beat the Dow" more times than not. They sell at the following year-end to capture profits and buy into the new group of "dogs" for the next year.

Expert Advice?

Some advice is good, much is bad. When prodded for advice, *Worth* magazine's staff humorously replied: *Buy low, sell high, unless you sell short, in which case you should still buy low and sell high, but in reverse.*

Will Rogers gave similar counsel: *Only buy stocks that go up in price. If they don't go up, don't buy them!*

A 1997 survey by the Securities Industry Association, revealed that *only 4% of experienced investors knew everything they needed to know to make good investment decisions and 81% said the securities industry should be doing more to educate them.*

It's amazing to think that only 4% of experienced investors (owning investments of $100,000 and more) were sufficiently knowledgeable investors! No wonder so many investors think they need help and depend on broker advice.

Betterness At Investing was written to help investors to discover for themselves what they need to know to be profitable do-it-yourself investors.

Foreign Investments

It is not necessary to balance portfolios with foreign stocks. It is safer, and profitable, to invest in American multi-national firms, such as Coca-Cola, GE, Dell, Microsoft, and others, that already have exposure in global markets.

Fundamental versus Technical Analysis

Fundamental Analysis focuses on a company's *financial health*. Technical Analysis exams *business activity*.

Fundamental Analysis studies a *company's value* -- earnings, dividends, sales, finances, and management. Fundamental analysts can avoid surprises by studying the balance sheet, fixed assets, current assets, stockholders equity, deferred taxes -- as reported in *Value Line* and *S&P*.

Technical Analysis is the *study of market factors*. Technical analysts use charts to seek breakout, downward and sideways movements that project trends. Technical analysts believe there are predictable cycles that influence trends. The Dow Theory was created to discover changes in market trends in support of technical analysis.

Can 1929 be repeated?

Modern controls prevent a repeat of 1929. In the current stock market a decline may seem severe but improved controls prevent disastrous consequences.

The financial fallout in 2008 was severe but nothing like the disaster of 1929 as the Federal Reserve released cash to prevent market failures. Exchanges now have "circuit breakers" to handle surges of large transactions. Trading is stopped when the Dow drops 300 points and again at 500.

Whenever the market drops, don't panic. If you don't sell you still have the same number of shares. You only lose money if you sell when value is less than cost.

Beware of margin loans. Limits on "margin accounts" assure payment of shares bought on margin when prices drop too low. Over-margined investors unable to cover losses caused much of the panic in 1929.

Trading volume is so much greater <u>the *percentage* of change</u> to shutdown the market must be greater than in 1929. A very large drop must occur.

A drop of 100 points in 1929 was 55% of the Dow! A movement of 100 is now only 1% of the Dow. <u>To recreate 1929 the Dow would have to drop over 5500 points!</u>

Market Index
An index monitors, controls, and reports price movements. The oldest index is the ***Dow Jones Industrial Average***® ***(DJIA)*** created in 1896 to track 12 firms. It now tracks 30 of <u>the best-capitalized industrial firms</u>. The Dow is price weighted to reflect higher priced member stocks. GE is the only stock continually listed since its beginning of the Dow over 100 years ago.

Standard & Poor 500 ***Index***® (S&P500) provides a wider view of market activity. It includes all exchanges weighted by capitalization (current price times number of outstanding shares).

Companies listed are heavily capitalized. Many funds track the S&P because it is the <u>most reflective of market trends</u>.

NYSE Composite Index® reflects NY Stock Exchange stocks weighted by market price times shares outstanding.

AMEX Market Value Index® weighted American Stock Exchange stocks. Also called ASE Index®.

NASDAQ OTC Index® -- tracks price of approximately 5000 stocks. Small-cap stocks are not included.

Value Line Index® is based on 1700 NYSE, AMEX, NASDAQ (over-the-counter), and Canadian Exchange stocks. Equal weight is given to each stock.

Wilshire 5000 Equity Index® all traded securities, weighted by market value (price times outstanding shares).

Russell 1000®-- largest capitalized stocks, 2000 -- next largest cap, *Russell 3000*® tracks all 3000.

Stock Exchanges

Exchanges evolved after the Revolutionary War to trade U.S. stocks previously traded on the London Exchange. An exchange provides invaluable service.

If stocks were traded between a company and investors, the company would be swamped. Exchanges "make a market" by setting prices and handle buy/sell transactions. Exchanges protect buyers and sellers.

NASDAQ -- National Association of Security Dealers Automated Quotations®. Small emerging companies need a place to exchange (over-the-counter) non-NYSE stocks. Unlike the NYSE, NASDAQ has no exchange center. It is computerized. Brokers call dealers for quotes to buy or sell.

AMEX® -- *American Stock Exchange*® -- a solution for equities that do not qualify for NYSE or NASDAQ. Companies listed are usually younger firms, thus, may be more volatile securities.

Commodity Exchanges – CBOT; CME
The Chicago Board of Trade bring together sellers and buyers of commodities. Sellers want to hedge the price of future crops. Buyers bet on the future price. The attraction is the low cost of contracts. A few hundred dollars will buy a future contract that could be worth thousands of dollars. This is a different market than stock ownership and requires extensive research before attempting to invest. The Chicago Mercantile Exchange (CME) was organized to expand the trading options of the CBOT.

Stock Options – for a small fee investors can wager that a stock price will fall (put) or grow (call). <u>If you have the time and willing to takes some small loses</u> large gains are possible. Seek broker assistance!

Summary Chapter 15 -- Miscellaneous Topics

- Non-essential information needlessly interferes with investment decisions. Print or television stories are not essential to routine investing, yet attract the interest of people hoping to better understand investing.

- Whatever their status, investors should always concentrate on safety, growth and yield -- as with established and proven growth companies.

- As many economic predications are not reliable, rely on the facts as reported in *Value Line®* and *Motley Fools®*.

- There is hope that science can solve what economists cannot -- a reliable formula for economic condition.

- The most successful investors have a positive attitude, have a tolerance for risk, and aim for high total returns on their investments.

SUMMARY – SECTION I
INVESTING FOR WEALTH

- The purpose of investing is to create wealth.

- The best way to create wealth is to:
  - ✓ Invest long-term in stocks, mutual funds, or ETF
  - ✓ Invest in quality growth
  - ✓ Maximize the *total* return on investments.

- Maximize by:
  - ✓ Reducing share cost.
  - ✓ Reinvesting dividends.
  - ✓ Capture compounding by holding long-term

- Myth and fear dissuade people from investing or investing wisely. Wise investors study *Value Line®*.

- An investment plan that supports the *Rules for Profitable Investing©* disciplines investors to:
  - ✓ *Never* buy or sell without researching *Value Line*
  - ✓ *Never* react emotionally to sensationalist news
  - ✓ *Never* own too many different company stocks
  - ✓ *Never* be content with low returns
  - ✓ *Never* fail to measure *percentages of gain*
  - ✓ *Never* hold poor performing stocks

- **<u>Wise investors</u>:**
  - ✓ Buy equities that control a business market.
  - ✓ Practice "*the Rules of Profitable Investing*."
  - ✓ Keep records in an *Investment Workbook*.
  - ✓ Research *Value Line®*.
  - ✓ Maximize total returns.
  - ✓ Qualify results as "percentages."
  - ✓ Do not panic
  - ✓ Exploit chances to buy at lower cost.

- **Why not fund Social Security with stock investments?** Long-term, SS would excel from growth and compounding -- which could multiply to millions of dollars -- at no cost to the government.

- **People who fail to create wealth because of fear and belief in myths should <u>learn the truth and profit</u> from investing.**

> *A prudent man foresees difficulties*
> *and prepares for them.*
> *A simpleton goes blindly,*
> *and suffers the consequences.*
> **Proverbs 22:3**

SECTION II

INVESTING WORKSHEETS

Strategies for Planning

Investment Plan

Selection Criteria

Selection Comparison

Investment Workbook

Stock Ownership Records

Portfolio Summary

Worksheets may be downloaded from:

http://www.bobdeneen.com

Strategies for Planning [©]

Successful investors do not let the hype of "experts" confuse or scare them. Nor do they invest blindly. The best strategies evolve from a mindset that supports the KISS principle and stays focused on planned goals to take advantage of compounded value. Decisions based on information researched in *ValueLine Surveys*™ reduce risk potential and increase reward potential.

The *Wall Street Journal Lifetime Guide to Money* recommends buying insurance as the first step in managing your money as it creates an immediate estate for your family. If needed, it can provide an emergency source of cash in later years – perhaps for providing the down-payment on a home or college.

The WSJ advocates that investors must take control: *Stay focused and avoid complex financial strategies and products when simpler ones will do. Most people can accomplish a great deal for themselves – with only limited time and effort – if they just remember to keep it simple.*

The WSJ book also warns against letting financial jargon or complex strategies steer investors off their own easy-to-follow investment plan. Things to focus on include the following:

☞ Don't select stock on a single criteria. Match criteria for the best potential return.

☞ Balance risk and volatility. Seek a low Beta as listed in *Value Line*®.

☞ Seek stocks with higher yields.

☞ Choose a DRIP stock.

☞ Buy at a practical price. Target a price range that is affordable for routine deposits.

☞ Feel satisfied with each investment. Do you like the company, its products, services? Satisfied to accumulate and hold shares long-term?

☞ Consider each stock investment as the most important investment you will ever make.

☞ **Aim for higher than average annual return** -- why own a stock with mediocre potential? Higher returns are available; find them in *Value Line*®.

☞ **Consider future circumstances**. Invest as much as possible when young. Near retirement consider trading some stocks for bonds.

☞ **Use the following Investment-Aides©** ....

Readers of *Betterness At Investing* have permission to copy the preceding Investment-Aides© for use in making <u>personal</u> investment decisions.

INVESTMENT PLAN ©

I/We _____, plan to invest $____ each
month to routinely acquire shares of a growth company until at
least 100 shares are owned before considering to buy equity in
another company, and:

- The goal is to capture 15% to 17% <u>or more</u> in total return.
Shares below this goal will be replaced.

- *Value Line*® will be reviewed before buying/selling.

- Share value will be maximized by buying company-direct,
dollar-cost-averaging (DCA), re-investing dividends (DRIP),
and holding long-term to exploit the compounding of value.

- If money is needed in an emergency, a short-term margin
loan will be considered rather than selling shares. Retained
value of shares will grow in value faster than cost of loan.

- Shares won't be sold in panic during downturns. If possible,
extra shares will be bought to increase holdings at lower cost.

- Recording purchases, dividends, splits, sales, taxes, and fees
will be kept up-to-date in an Investment Workbook.

- No one else is to manage or alter this plan.

Signed: _____ Date:_____

Note: A printable copy of this worksheet may be downloaded
from:
www.boddeneen.com/Worksheet/InvestmentPlan.htm

Selection Criteria

Stock Symbol: _____ _____ _____

Growth Potential _____ _____ _____
Value Line rating, or rate as: A (best), B (good), C (marginal)

Products:
Sales growth _____ _____ _____
Marketshare _____ _____ _____
Innovations _____ _____ _____

Management
Experience _____ _____ _____
Performance _____ _____ _____
Ethics _____ _____ _____

Dividend
Payment consistency _____ _____ _____
DRIP -- Yes/No _____ _____ _____

Timeliness _____ _____ _____

Safety _____ _____ _____

P/E Ratio _____ _____ _____

Capital Rating _____ _____ _____

Summary:	A	B	C	1	2	3	DRIP	P/E

Stock Symbol:

_____

_____

SELECTION COMPARISON ®
(*Value Line*® data, unless otherwise noted)

	Company	Company	Company
Stock Symbol	_____	_____	_____
Date	_____	_____	_____
Share Price	$_____	$_____	$_____

Financial

Rate (B++ to A)	_____	_____	_____
Timeliness*(1-3)	_____	_____	_____
Safety *(1- 3)	_____	_____	_____
Div.Yield *	_____%	_____%	_____%
DRIP?	_____	_____	_____
P/E Ratio *	_____	_____	_____
Price Stability *	_____	_____	_____
Price Growth	_____	_____	_____
Earnings *	_____	_____	_____
Beta	_____	_____	_____
Expect Growth	_____%	_____%	_____%
Est. Return	_____%	_____%	_____%

Individual Stock Record ©

Buy Date	#Shs.	Price	Cost	Dividend.......	
_____	_____	$_____	$_____	$_____	_____%
_____	_____	$_____	$_____	$_____	_____%
_____	_____	$_____	$_____	$_____	_____%

Record of Stock Splits:

Date _____	_____	_____	_____
# Shs:_____	_____	_____	_____
Value $_____	_____	_____	_____

Betterness At Investing

INVESTMENT WORKBOOK ©

- **Investment Plan:** Review and evaluate.

- **Rules for Profitable Investing** ©
  1. Have an investment plan
  2. Invest in quality growth companies
  3. Make your own decisions based on research
  4. Buy routinely to maximize *total return*
  5. Monitor and measure performance
  6. Adjust holdings -- if potential changes

- **Timely records:** Stocks bought, sold, dividends reinvested, stock splits. Update records each quarter, if not monthly.

- **Quarterly Statements:** Shareholders receive a statement of holdings each quarter to confirm purchases, sales, dividends, and splits. Store current and year-end statements in your workbook.

- **Selection Notes:** Store *Value Line* summaries of stocks bought or considered. Include research notes. Use a "Watch List" as practice portfolio and of stocks to consider.

- **Practice Portfolios:** Pretend to buy and track as real transactions. Test your skill, make mistakes, generate imaginary gains, and prove strategies. Some experts suggest practicing for six months before attempting the real thing.

- **Performance Reviews:** store spreadsheet record of each stock to confirm worth. Measure gain/loss in percentages.

- **Form 1099 Statements:** Investors annually receive Form 1099 to reporting dividend and interest to IRS. Same form used to report capital gains credited to mutual fund accounts.

STOCK OWNERSHIP RECORD ©

Date_____ **Company**_____
Symbol_____
Account #_____
Transfer Agent/800#_____

Date Buy/Sell	# Shs	$ Price	$ Fees	%. Div.	Total Shares	Total Value
_____	____	_____	____	____	____	$_____
_____	____	_____	____	____	____	$_____
_____	____	_____	____	____	____	$_____
_____	____	_____	____	____	____	$_____
_____	____	_____	____	____	____	

Dividend Received	**$/Value**	**#/Shares**
Date_____	_____	_____
Date _____	_____	_____
Date_____	_____	_____

Record of Splits

Date _____ # Shares:_____ $/sh_____
Date _____ # Shares:_____ $/sh_____
Date _____ # Shares:_____ $/sh_____

Notes:

PORTFOLIO SUMMARY©

Date_____

Company	Symbol	# Shares	Price (sh)	Value
_____	____	____	$_____	$_____
_____	____	____	$_____	$_____
_____	____	____	$_____	$_____
_____	____	____	$_____	$_____
			TOTAL VALUE	**$_____**

ANNUAL GROWTH

Year 1   Gain_____% Gain $_____
Year 2   Gain_____% Gain $_____
Year 3   Gain_____% Gain $_____
Year 4   Gain_____% Gain $_____
Year 5   Gain_____% Gain $_____

Notes:

_____
_____
_____
_____
_____
_____

CB✧BO

APPENDIX

BIBLIOGRAPHY & REFERENCES

Buffettology: The Previously Unexplained Techniques That Made Warren Buffett the World's Most Famous Investor, Mary Buffett and David Clark

Buying Stocks Without A Broker, Charles B. Carlson

Common Stocks and Uncommon Profits, Philip A. Fisher

How to Invest $50 - $50,000, Nancy Dunnan, 1993

Learn to Earn, Peter Lynch & John Rothschild

No-Load Stocks, Charles Carlson

The Intelligent Investor, Benjamin Graham

The Moneypaper® Guide to direct investing

The Motley Fool Investment Guide, David & Tom Gardner

The Wall Street Journal Lifetime Guide to Money, the WSJ's Personal Finance Staff

The Warren Buffett Way: Investment Strategies of the World's Greatest Investor, Robert G. Hagstrom, Jr.

Value Line Investment Surveys

Warren Buffett Speaks, Janet Lowe

NEWSLETTERS, JOURNALS, WEBSITES

ASSOCIATIONS:
AAII, American Association of Individual Investors ®
1-800/428-2244 625 N. Michigan Ave., Chicago, ILL 60611

NAIC National Association of Investment Clubs ®
PO Box 220, Royal Oak, MI   48068-0220

AAII Journal
American Association of Individual Investors

Directory of Dividend Reinvestment Plans
7412 Calumet Avenue, Hammond, IN 46324
219/931-6480

The Moneypaper Guide to Dividend Reinvestment
 --new investors should request information
Temper of the Times Communications   914/381-5400

The Value Line Investment Survey®
Value Line Publishing, Inc.
 220 East 42nd St, N.Y. N.Y. 10017-5891
 1-800/833-004

Dow Industrial Average and Index
www.djindexes.com/jsp/industrialAverages.jsp?sideMenu=true.html

The Dow List -- symbol, price, dividend. Dow 10; Dow 5
www.djindexes.com/downloads/selectionlists/DJDow510_Selection.xls

Smart Money Magazine
ww.smartmoney.com/mag/index.cfm?story=update-april01

Motley Crew -- www.fool.com

GLOSSARY

a – in stock listings:
    a1 - indicates cash payment in addition to regular dividend.
    a2 - yield; may include gain/loss in money market mutual funds.

accumulation – purchasing routinely. (*Dollar-cost-averaging*)

active trading -- active buying/selling. Attempting to produce above-average returns to beat market averages.

advisory fee -- fee for investment management or advice.

allocation -- spreading investment over time and investments.

AMEX; ASE -- American Stock Exchange ®

annualized -- variable return converted to an annual rate. A 1% dividend in one-quarter (3 mos.) is a 4% annualized yield.

annual report -- 'corporate' performance report. The 10-K (complete financial data) issued separately.

annual fee -- management fees, as with 12b-1 fee. Does not include 'load' fee. 'No-load' funds may have annual fees.

asset allocation -- spreading investments over various securities -- half in stocks; half in bonds (50/50) -- or 60/40

asset play -- targeting assets of stock depressed by low earnings. Investor calculates more value than current share price. (asset value)

asset value -- a stock whose price does not reflect the higher value of a firm's assets.

authorized stock -- number of shares corporation authorized to issue, as defined in articles of incorporation, and as approved by shareholders.

b -- when in dividend column of newspaper indicates payment of a <u>stock</u> dividend <u>in addition to</u> <u>cash</u> dividend.

bear market -- negative period of depressed share prices. Usually exists when there is a 20% decline that remains for an extended time period.

beta -- measure of volatility of stock in relation to general market. Lower beta safer the investment. Standard is '1'.

blue chip -- exceptional quality stock of a well-financed company with a history of consistent earnings and dividends.

book value -- value of assets less liabilities/debts. Book value/share is value divided by number of outstanding shares.

book value per share -- common stockholder equity per share; book value or book.

broker-dealer -- broker that takes ownership position in share trade.

bull -- bullish; positive, upward trend. An investor who believes market will move upward -- as in a bull market.

capital gain -- proceeds that exceed cost when stock is sold. Capital gains of mutual funds are recorded yearly; thus shareholders are tax liable.

capital stock -- shares of corporation (preferred & common).

cash flow --   net income, plus depreciation and uncommon charges. An important measure of financial strength.

cash flow/share -- divide cash flow by number of outstanding shares. Optional measure of earnings per share.

certificate -- evidence of ownership; contains name of issuer, owner, number of shares. Eliminated by electronic records.

CEO   -- chief executive officer; usually President; may be Chairman.

churn/churning -- excessive trading of an account by a broker or an account manager.

CUSIP -- identification numbers assigned to all registered stocks and bonds by Committee on Uniform Securities Identification Procedures.

custodian account -- account managed by someone other than owner; as minors or people not wanting or unable to manage investments.

common stock -- stock that has no preference to distribution of assets or dividends; usually has voting rights. Common stock shareholders are owners of a corporation.

compound return -- annual rate of return from stock when dividends are reinvested at the same rate of return.

contrarian -- investor against common expectations. Seeks unpopular stock as a method of finding undervalued stocks.

cum dividend -- stocks that can be bought <u>with dividend</u> paid to the buyer versus ex-dividend (dividend goes to seller).

d -- indicates a new low for the year in stock listings.

discretionary account -- gives power of attorney to broker -- allows broker to buy/sell at their discretion. See "<u>churning</u>".

Dividend Ratios -- Yield versus Payout. <u>Yield</u> equals dividend paid divided by market price. <u>Payout</u> is divided by <u>earnings per share</u>.

dividend yield -- dividend divided by share price. If $50 per share and dividend is $2.00, the yield is 4% ($50/$2).

Dow Jones Averages ® -- **Index** of Dow Jones & Company, publisher of *Wall Street Journal* and *Dow Jones Averages.*

e --indicates dividend declared and paid in prior 12 months.

earning power -- expected yield under best conditions.

earnings -- income of a business, usually after-tax income.

earnings per share (EPS) -- net income, less dividends to preferred shareholders, divided by outstanding shares of common stock. May be called *income per share.*

earnings-price ratio (E/P ratio) -- divide projected earnings/share by current market. A low E/P ratio anticipates higher than average earnings.

equity -- partial ownership of a corporation; a share of stock

ex-dividend -- stock that trades without right to receive next dividend payment. Usually because purchase made after dividend was declared.

fallen angel -- stock that has declined in value; lost investor interest.

family trust -- a trust for the purpose of passing assets to heirs; may be other than a surviving spouse.

fiduciary -- person, executor, organization, entrusted with property. Expected to act in best interests of asset owner.

financial rating -- rated (A, A-, B) by professional analysts; as in *Value Line* and S&P summaries.

financial planner -- counsels investors about financial status, goals. Investors must be cautious of 'planners' who sell product. Should pay only for services. Insurance agents and brokers may not be unbiased.

fundamentals -- basic economic, financial, operating factors that influence the success of a business and the price of its stock.

future value -- amount a specific sum will grow in a given time. $1,000 has future value of $1,150 in one year from annual return of 15%.

gain -- income from sale of stock (selling price minus cost). Cost includes commissions and fees. Keep a record of all costs and earnings.

growth stock -- above average increases in earnings. A high PE ratios; experience wide swings in market price.

identify shares -- distinguishing shares to be sold. Identify shares to control profit or loss. Identify shares with highest cost to minimize tax on capital gain.

institutional investor -- may be insurance company, investment firm, mutual fund that invests large sums. Has increasing impact on trading as movement of huge blocks of stock causes wider price fluctuations.

intrinsic value -- theoretical price of stock when properly priced in the market; core of fundamental analysis. Also called Investment Value.

January indicator -- tendency for market activity in January to set the yearly trend.

joint account -- owned by two or more entities (people; trust), in which ownership automatically reverts to survivor(s).

L -- in stock listings indicates a stock has reached a new 52- week low.

large-cap stocks -- stock of big corporations with considerable retained earnings and common stock outstanding. Generally listed in Dow Jones.

limit order -- fixes highest price paid for a buy order.

liabilities -- current and future claims against a business.

load -- sales fee when funds are purchased. Reduces the investment return.

management fee -- percentage of the value of the managed portfolio.

margin account -- buying of securities on credit through a brokerage account. Usually limited to 50% of current market value of securities.

market capitalization -- share price times number of shares outstanding.

market order -- executing an order at the exchange price.

microcap -- companies under $250 million in capitalization. Smallcap limited to firms under $150 million.

model -- mathematical formula; computer spreadsheet; abstraction.

n --indicates a new listing in transaction tables.

NASDAQ ® -- National Association of Securities Dealers Automated Quotation System operated by NASD, exchange for unlisted securities.

NAV -- net asset value per share. Calculation of a mutual fund's share value of assets minus liabilities divided by number of outstanding shares. The price an investor receives when selling shares back to the fund.

net income -- income after expenses and taxes have been deducted. Net income per share is same as earnings per share.

net profit margin -- net margin: after tax net income divided by sales.

NYSE ® -- New York Stock Exchange, founded in 1792 is the largest exchange. To be listed a corporation must have at least 2000 shareholders of 100 or more shares; a minimum of 1.1 million publicly held shares; and a market value of $18 million.

Nifty fifty -- fifty large growth stocks favored by institutional investors. Have record of rising earnings and dividends.

odd lot -- unit of trade of less than 100 shares of stock; incurs markup of commissions to compensate from smaller volume.

owners' equity -- owners' equity interest in business assets.

P -- indicates initial dividend in stock transaction tables.

P/E ratio -- price earnings ratio. Earnings yield divided by current share price. Relative P/E is relative to other stocks in the same industry.

Pf -- indicates a preferred stock; sometimes "pr".

preferred stock -- equity ownership that has precedence over common stock for earnings and assets. Usually pays fixed dividend. Limited appeal to individual growth investors. Can be recalled.

portfolio -- specific group of investments belonging to the owner. Owner may be a group (club), individual, or trust.

Profitability (EPS) -- earnings per share of common stock

P/SR ratio -- price-sales ratio, compares the stock price with sales per share; or the total market value with total revenue.

P/A ratio -- price to asset ratio compares price with book value/share.

r -- used in the dividend column of stock transaction tables to indicate amount of dividend in proceeding 12 months.

Relative strength -- stock's price strength relative to index or general market.

Return on equity -- net income divided by stockholder's equity.

Reverse stock split -- decrease in number of shares outstanding; giving investors fewer but higher priced shares, as a one-for-two stock split.

ROI-- return on investment = net profit after taxes divided by assets

round lot -- 100 shares; regular trading unit. Odd lot is less.

Rule of 72 -- formula for approximating number of years for investment to double. Calculated by dividing 72 by the annual rate of return.

Short sales -- advance sale in anticipation of a price decline

stop-loss order -- similar to limit order; fixes lowest acceptable selling price, and will remain until canceled, unless specified.

Schedule D -- tax form listing gains and losses from selling.

Screen -- filters information based on selected data. Example: stocks with a dividend with 2% or higher yield.

SEC   -- Securities Exchange Commission

Securities Acts -- Act of 1933 prohibits certain practices. Act of 1934 gave SEC authority to regulate trading, and the Federal Reserve authority over credit buying of securities.

These two acts prevent the repeat of events and activities that occurred in the crash of 1929. Act of 1970 established Securities Investor Protection Corporation (SIPC) to correct unstable practices. SIPC insures losses ($100,000 per investor) from insolvency of security firms.

Short sale -- selling stock before owned in anticipation of price drop. Investor expects to buy at the lower cost before delivery to cover sale.

Small-cap stock -- small capitalization stock with limited number of shares or capitalization of less than $1 billion. Russell 2000 Index.

Specialist -- stock exchange trader who is a 'market maker' in certain securities. Trades on exchange floor among other specialists. *Specialist activity may not appear logical in relation to the economy or general market conditions.*

Standard & Poor's (S&P) ® -- advisory reports and publishes guides.

S&P 500 Index (S&P 500) -- Index of 400 industrial, 40 utilities, 20 transportation and 40 financial firms.

Stock option -- option to buy/sell specific number of shares at a fixed price.

Super DRIP -- direct purchase of stock, commission-free.

T -- in listings, indicates market value at date of dividend

Treasuries -- bonds issued through the Treasury Department and backed by U.S. government. Can be bought direct to avoid broker commissions.

Treasury bond -- long-term interest bearing Treasury debt.

Treasury note -- short-term (1-10 year) interest debt of U.S.

u -- indicates stock price has reached a new 52-week high.

V -- in stock listings indicates firm is in bankruptcy.

Warrant -- a security that permits owner to buy a specified number of shares at a predetermined price.

Whilshire 5000 Equity Index ® -- measure of stock prices of all stock on NYSE and AMEX, plus active over-the-counter (OTC) stock.

Ww --indicates stock is traded with warrants.

X -- indicates stock is traded ex-dividend

z -- volume reported is actual number, and not round-lots.

INDEX

A

B

I_____

J_____X

N_____

O_____

P

Q

R

reinvested dividends (DRIP) – 19, 26-27, 38, 55-57, 60, 66, 70, 81, 92, 102, 106, 110

resources (*time, information, money)* – 23, 35

research – 3, 10, 18-19, 24, 29-31, 35, 45, 47, 50, 63, 66, 78, 90-93, 96, 102, 131

retirement – 94, 97

reward – 17-19, 26-27, 30, 35-36, 52, 54-55, 69

risk – 11, 17-19, 26, 30-31, 35-36, 41-42, 44, 47, 52, 54, 58, 61, 84, 91, 97

Rogers, Will -- 86

Rukeyser, Lou -- 128

rules – (Investing Rules) -- 12, 22, 28, 32, 60, 68, 92, 102

Rule of 72 -- "doubling of value" – 56, 116

S_____

Safety® – 29, 31-33, 35-36, 40-46, 62, 91, 100-101

SEC – 116-117

selection – 5, 20-22, 26, 29-32, 34-36, 38, 40, 43-44, 46-47, 49, 53, 64, 94, 100-102, 106, 129, 133

Selection Comparison -- 101

Selection Criteria -- 100

selling – 23-24, 46, 66-67, 99, 107, 112, 116, 117

total return – 4, 10, 17-20, 22-24, 26, 28-29, 31, 33, 37,
40, 43, 50, 55, 60, 61, 67, 77, 91, 92-93,
99, 102, 132-133

Trusts – 75, 83-84

U_____

undervalued stocks – (see Dogs of the Dow)-- 85

V_____

value – 14, 16-17, 20-23, 25-28, 33-34, 48-39, 45, 48,
55-60, 62-63, 67, 69-70, 75-80, 82, 85, 87, 89,
96, 99, 101, 103-104, 107-108, 111-115, 118,
132-135

Value Line Investment Surveys© -- 2-4, 12, 17-20, 23,
26, 29-36, 40-46, 48, 61-62, 64, 66, 68, 72, 78-79,
87, 89, 91-93, 97, 99-102, 105-106, 111, 124

Vanguard – 30, 38, 48-50, 52-53

W_____

Wall Street – 14, 45

Wall Street Journal – 3, 45-46, 105, 110

watchlist – (also see practice portfolio) -- 40

websites (useful) -- 106

XYZ_____

ଓଓ✧ଃଠ

> *We become what we practice.*
> *To create wealth,*
> *practice betterness at investing.*

 **About the Author**

For most of his career, Bob Deneen has been a businessperson -- in sales, marketing, a chief executive, and entrepreneur. He learned the value of planning and setting objectives -- which he applies to his books: Betterness In Life, Betterness In Business, and Betterness At Investing.

For many years his investments were limited to his business ventures. Then, in 1995, he discovered the fantastic potential of stocks when his mother reviewed with him her investing experience. Her do-it-yourself results inspired him to research strategies of well-known investors.

After thousands of hours of research he discovered two things. One, his mother used most strategies of the renowned experts. Two, a practical guidebook was needed for beginning investors, investors desiring a higher return, and investors who doubted the benefits of owning stock – all of which are reviewed in Betterness At Investing.

An advocate of positive thinking, Bob believes that anyone can become a wealthy investor -- if they believe they can.

EPILOGUE

Investors who dispel doubt and fear about investing – and apply the strategies and aides within this book – should be able to create substantial wealth.

Successful investors have a positive mindset and are effective managers of their holdings. Leaving investments to chance is not effective management. It is important to <u>monitor the performance</u> of your holdings.

Economic growth may not be as robust as in the past, but <u>substantial profits can still be captured</u> by applying *value-adding tactics* to maximize the total return on investments.

Realistic investors don't waste time on useless information. They don't try to understand every complex factor about the stock market but <u>focus on creating wealth</u> from the stocks they own. They practice the KISS principle.

How can investors sift through the glut of media hype about the stock market and the economy? They can't! Even economists don't agree and none know exactly how the market will perform. Aside from catastrophic events, the market reflects the average of all listed stocks.

A few simple strategies however allow individuals to create wealth strategies by investing in growth stocks that excel as market leaders – and exploit the magic of compounding.

Other than winning the lottery or inheriting money, stock investing is the best way to create wealth! Time magazine (1/23/10) referred to a survey that asked: *Which tends to have the highest growth over periods of time as long as 18 years?* The answer was stocks.

While some stocks increase and others shrink in value, the most important thing for investors to monitor is the performance of the stocks they own. Study *ValueLine Survey* newsletters and charts – select from the list of 100 best stocks to own.

Being able to remain calm when the market is crashing is not an easy task. The "chicken little" syndrome to take flight can influence anyone. Do-it-yourself investors who are confident about their stock selections are not likely to panic by staying focused on:
- ✓ Strategies proven successful and profitable
- ✓ Investing in quality growth companies
- ✓ Acquiring extra shares
- ✓ Maximizing total return
- ✓ Capturing the magic of compounding

Markets always recover after a crash and climb higher. They always have, and always will because the economy continually expands.

The United States has the same economic elements that existed before the recent recession – which while slowly recovering will eventually achieve a higher prosperity..

The danger is that fearful investors will slow down the recovery by staying out of the market – and we will all miss the potential gain in growth.

Fortunately, the forces that drive economic growth can overcome this obstacle. It is also fortunate that everyone can share in economic growth.

The wonderful thing about investing is that it is freely available to anyone who is motivated to create wealth.

Anyone can achieve betterness at investing by taking advantage of the unique buying opportunities and the compounding of value.

THE END

———————

୧✦୨

Betterness At Investing

www.ingramcontent.com/pod-product-compliance
Lightning Source LLC
Chambersburg PA
CBHW051538170526
45165CB00002B/783